I0620624

Exquisite Egyptian
Belly Dance Moves

Fun • Fitness • Femininity

Khalidah Kali

Exquisite Egyptian Belly Dance Moves

Copyright © 2024 by Khalidah Kali

For information contact :

Khalidahsdance.com

info@shepublishingllc.com

www.shepublishingllc.com

Book Cover and Title Page design by Michelle Phillips of CHELLD3 3D VISUALIZATION AND DESIGN

Library of Congress Control Number: 2024952276

ISBN : 978-1-953163-78-3 (paperback)

First Edition : November 2024

10 9 8 7 6 5 4 3 2 1

Table of Contents

DISCLAIMER

The reader, herein, must agree, understand, give up, and hold harmless all hurt, harm, or danger, to Khalidah Kali and Khalidah's North African Dance Experience (KNADE).

Khalidah Kali and KNADE are Not responsible for past, current, or future injuries, losses, or damages as a result of using or performing dance moves or using food suggestions contained within this publication or executing any business, whatsoever, with Khalidah Kali, and/or KNADE.

It would be best never to attempt to treat or diagnose yourself or start a new exercise program without a health professional's advice and assistance. No statement in this publication should be construed as a claim for cure, treatment, or prevention of any disease or allergy. It is also important to note that you should accept mainstream medical methods. Learn about your condition, and don't be afraid to ask questions.

Feel free to get second and even third opinions from qualified health care professionals. It is a sign of wisdom, not cowardice, to seek more knowledge through your active participation.

Khalidah Kali in Egypt at Giza Pyramids

FORWARD

(Forward)

"Khalidah, you are on top of your genre.

Think about it!"

Najwa

Founder and 1st Artistic Director of Najwa Dance Corps

Chicago's Grand Iconic Queen Mother of Dance

"As a dancer, Khalidah Kali is charismatic, and sensuous.

I have watched Khalidah teach Egyptian 'Belly' Dancing while enriching the lives of her students and making them feel as luscious females.

The dancers who perform with Khalidah have illuminated their lives bringing out the best in themselves.

Khalidah Kali takes her form of dance and uses it to bring out the best in dancers … they are the better for knowing her.

I Appreciate you SISTAR. What you offer is vital and important.

I appreciate you."

Darlene Blackburn,
Chicago's Grand Iconic Queen Mother of Dance

DEDICATIONS & ACKNOWLEDGMENTS

(Dedications and Acknowledgments)
GREETINGS AND SALUTATIONS!

To the Most High.

To my Late Mother, Temple Payton, and to my Late Father,

James Hickman, Sr.

To All my students and readers of this book, past, present, and future.

To Mrs. Shenitha Burton of S.H.E. Publishing!

There's no way this book is possible without You!

To my Genius Curator & New Media Content Producer,

Mr. Floyd Webb, who caused breakthrough with book for me!

To My Husband, Theodore Evans, for his extreme reliability, love, and assistance in everything I pursue.

To My Late Husband, El Hajj, Farid Al-Taqi, Sr., who was pivotal in life, in keeping my dance pursuits as authentic as possible while working diligently to bring my dance dreams to reality.

To my Very Big Dance Teacher in New York City,

Ms. Carolina Dinicu "Rocky," "Morocco," "Aunty Rocky," for her huge encouragement and spirit-of-inclusivity, and great teachings during her huge and magnificent dance conferences in NYC, and for her dance study tours for which I attended on many occasions, in Egypt, Morocco, and Istanbul, Turkey.

My gratitude is unending for her 60+ years of research and dance genius experience.

(Dedications and Acknowledgments)

To my dance business partner and student, Elaine Folashade' McGee-Wadiei, who has always been there for me, and the dance company, Khalidah's North African Dance Experience, Inc., for these 36+ years, for classes, rehearsals, performances, et cetera.

God, and Ms. Elaine are my Guiding Light," a light that always lets me know I'm on the "Right Track!"

This journey has been graced, because of God, and her presence, prayers, and encouragements!

I am extremely influenced by, and indebted to my personal dance teachers / dance leaders as follows:

Ms. Djalaal, Master Dance Teacher, Chicago, Illinois

The Late Jewel McLaurin, Chicago, Illinois

Darlene Blackburn, Chicago, IL

"Morocco" C. Varga Dinicu, New York City

Joel Hall and Joel Hall Dancers, Chicago, IL

Hema Rajagopalan, Natya Dance center, Chicago, IL

Mama Najwa of Najwa Dance Center, Chicago, IL

Mama Amaniyea, Emeritus Artistic Director

of Muntu Dance Theatre of Chicago

(Dedications and Acknowledgments)

Mama Ona Banks, my 1st Yoga Teacher when in my teens, and Godmother. She's, now, 98-years-young, in 2023!

Yoga Master, Yirser Ra Hotep Lawrence, Chicago, IL

Mama Somra El Nubia, St. Louis, MO

Mama Sofiyah Bailey of Hollywood, Florida Cultural Expressions

Mama Bernie Riley, a Chicago History Maker, and Godmother.

To my siblings, Cyndee Raymond McIntyre, James Jimi Hickman, Sister-in-law, Stephanie Jones, LaMont Payton, Billy and Ricky

You all are my "Rock!"

To Ms. Bridget Howard, committed friend and Dance Student Extraordinaire, Wild Genius, who works very hard without a complaint.

To All of my thousands of students, the community,

performance clients, grantors, and sponsors, past, present,

and future;

To everyone mentioned above, and beyond; your efforts, energy,

and support will Never be forgotten!

I AM, BECAUSE GOD IS, AND YOU ALL ARE!

TESTIMONIALS/MEDITATIONS

"Special K – Top Quality!"

Zenobia F. B.

"Les Brown has nothing on Khalidah!"

L. Frank

"Absolutely love this woman. Not only a master of teaching the Egyptian Belly Dance, and its beautiful art form (including my favorite of playing the finger cymbals), but also Khalidah is very knowledgeable and deeply spiritual, in tune with self, physical health, spiritual health, emotional health, women's health, knowledge, history, healing. Her aura is strong, calm, and full of light. Her words and advice still stick with me. Love her. She IS Fabulousness!"

Nicole of NYC

*"Everyday I go to Khalidah's class,
I get deep-down feelings of cleanliness, healthiness, and beauty."*

Beverly H.

"Found Khalidah's class to be a very inspirational and spiritual experience. She spent time not only instructing, but sharing her knowledge of Africa and the origins of the dances. There was a connection between women and

Mother Earth. I would love to have this experience again."

Kathleen

*"The Class is excellent! It's an exciting experience.
Camaraderie with ladies is perfect as well."*

Maryam H.

*"I enjoy Khalidah's class. It's better than any pill I could take.
At 70, it's a joy to move my body. Blessings to the Instructor."*

R. King

"This North African Dance Class is a Blessing from the Most High."

Sabra A.

*"Thank You for all your positivity.
Khalidah has a great Spirit, which motivates me to try."*

Essie B.

*"She is a Queen Mother of Wisdom and Peace. I am in awe of her zeal,
strength and tenacity for her dance family and life."*

Tess W.

"Everything is in Divine Order."

S. Suluki

"I feel love, peace, power, and wealth-in-abundance in the class."

Maisha B.

"Khalidah's class is relaxing, yet energetic. I enjoy the gracefulness of the class, and its principles. It helps me with flexibility, endurance, and strength. Khalidah is forever dedicated."

Ameedah

"My experience with Khalidah's Egyptian Belly Dance is awesome!

The class offers a good-fun workout, while focusing on the beauty and art of femininity. Khalidah is absolutely the best! She is a very positive influence on everyone, and just an all-around great person. So, if you are thinking of joining a belly dance class, I would highly recommend Khalidah's Egyptian Belly Dance Class. You won't be disappointed!"

Clarice E.

"EXQUISITE, ENCYCLOPEDIC, ENTHRALLING"
Mama Asantewaa of Philadelphia, (MIT Scholar)

"I thoroughly enjoyed the class. Khalidah has such a positive spirit, and provides not only a fun, up-beat Belly Dance class, but, provides positive lessons that I will carry and incorporate in my life."
Deana T.

"I feel more in touch with my feminine energy after every class. I walk taller, smile brighter, move more gracefully. Her classes are not only great for the body, it's good for the soul.

Chineze M.

"Khalidah is the Truth! I love how I radiate after our sessions. I feel so rich when I come to class. So very full!"
Dominique

"I truly enjoyed my class today! Khalidah was wonderful; very patient, and encouraging. She connected body and spirit to the dance. I feel I traveled to another continent."
Ekael

"This class has been so energizing. It's an oasis in the week to be able to show-up, dance, and feel recharged by the circle of positive feminine energy. I've enjoyed learning your dance moves."
Ms. Erin

"I'm truly grateful. You're a dedicated, knowledgeable, motivated, spirit-driven teacher bringing exceptional life enhancing knowledge to all who attend your classes! I thank you for sharing your passion to enhance women's well-being."
Denise King

INTRODUCTION

(Introduction)

GREETINGS AND SALUTATIONS!!

Dearest Reader:

Each dance movement chapter consists of:

1. Name of movement
2. An affirmation
3. Detailed description of movement
4. Health benefits of each featured movement

- P L U S. –

* **Testimonials**

* **Amazing pictures**

* **Details of how to use and "play" finger cymbals**

* **A beautiful description of how to dance with veils, and perform beautiful dance combinations with veils**

* **Nutritional value and ingredients of healthy foods and healthy drinks**

* **Herbal Actions**

* **List of Affirmations**

* **Books and Resources**

* **"About the Author" Pages**

* **Brief history and Author's bio on back cover**

(Introduction)

Once knowledge in this book is internalized, you acquire fun, weight loss/weight management, different types of fitness, anxiety and stress relief, feelings of sacred sensuality/femininity, et cetera, all in a healthy, wholistic, and safe way!

Most movements, in this book, are seen in many dances worldwide.

The only components that differentiate Egyptian moves from other movements are the timing, intention, speed, masculine or feminine

use of energy, amount of energy used, garments, music, dimensions of a movement, country-of-origin, placements, essence, etcetera.

In other words, it depends on where dance is globally that changes these components. However, the movements are basically the same globally, universally, especially in indigenous/ancient populations.

The words, "Belly Dance" are an American misnomer.

The movements herein are movements I've studied, on location, in

Africa, (Egypt/Kemet) many times, (over a dozen trips to Egypt) and in various states around the United States, and around-the-world such as Morocco, Istanbul, Turkey, India, Bangkok, Dubai, Saudi Arabia, and 40 plus countries.

Kemet is an ancient/indigenous term for Egypt.

Cairo, Egypt/Kemet, which is in Africa, has the main movement vocabulary of movements we're exploring in this book.

Egypt, in its antiquity, is where the foundation of the movements in this book originated.

Different elements of the movements change from country-to-country and region-to-region across north Africa.

3

(Introduction)

In honor and respect of the cultures of north Africa, it's not appropriate to call the whole of the dance, "Belly Dance," especially since every part of the body is used in the dance.

The following are names of a few of the dances that

Khalidah's North African Dance Experience (KNADE) perform.

You can now see appropriate/authentic names of dances.

English Name:	Arabic Name
Contemporary Egyptian	Raqs Sharqi
Traditional Egyptian	Raqs Baledi
Stick Dance	Raqs Al Asaya
Moroccan Women's Dance	Raqs Al Schikhatt
Saudi Arabian Dress Dance	Khaleegi; Raqs AL-Nasha
Egyptian Candelabra Dance	Raqs Al Shamadan
Moroccan Tea Tray Dance	Raqs AL Seniya
Tunisian Folk	Raqs AL Shabaya-JugDance
Nubian	Ollin Arageed

All movements contained herein have healthy benefits, and are effective for wholeness, wellness, fun, fitness, and sacred/divine femininity and sensuality.

The movements are of the oldest antiquity of dance.

(Introduction)

Spiritually speaking, the original intention of the dance was/is performed for prayer and healing of mind, body, spirit, emotions, and aligning with the sacred/divine feminine principle of enlightenment.

Movements are proven to be stress, anxiety relieving, and mood lifting, etc.

Consult a professional health physician before attempting practice of movements.

These movements are self-chiropractic, self-massaging of internal organs, healthy for female organs, aligning mind/body, nurturing, and calming of emotions.

Dance is meditation-in-motion, which enhances inner peace.

I'm confident you'll enjoy the movements!

Thank You for your personal investment in my beautiful book!

My prayer is that you receive grace and enhancement for your particular needs.

"Exquisite Egyptian 'Belly' Dance Moves,

Fun * Fitness * Femininity"

With Love, Yours in Egyptian Dance,

🌹 Khalidah Kali

FAVORITE EGYPTIAN
DANCE MOVEMENTS

FAVORITE EGYPTIAN DANCE MOVEMENTS
AS SEEN, ON LOCATION, IN EGYPT, AFRICA
BY KHALIDAH KALI

E N J O Y!

NOTE: Remember to consult your professional healthcare provider before starting any new exercise program.

Create repetitions of one, five, 10, 16, 20, or 30 repetitions on each side of body, depending on your level of strength and endurance for any movement or combinations of movements, while paying careful attention to level of energy so you don't overexert.

Creativity goes into infinity, when it comes to developing your own workout routine, choreography, et cetera.

For further details on how to better understand, and execute movements, simply purchase my dance instructional DVDs, hardcopy or virtually, and/or email me with any questions.

Please email me Before purchasing.
Khalidah@att.net.
www.khalidahsdance.com

Khalidah's North African Dance Experience
Providing a space to learn and practice!
www.khalidahsdance.com

Please See "Books and Resources" Page.

Thank You, so much, for your patience and understanding!

BASIC STRUCTURE
AND POSITION

(For all movement herein)

"Intelligence & Perfection are not a skill; it's an Attitude.
Your Attitude determines Your Altitude!"

Legs and feet are hip width apart.

Feet are very slightly left and right of center.

Weight distributed equally under the heels and balls of each foot.

Knees are slightly bent and relaxed.

The pelvis is neutral, and not slightly arched back or forward.

Use this natural stance at the start of each movement.

Torso (between top of shoulders and bottom of pelvis)

is in a naturally relaxed center-front position.

Use no tension in body during Basic Structure and Position.

BASIC STRUCTURE AND POSITION

(For all movements herein)

(*continued*)

Shoulders are relaxed and centered as you keep your shoulders even, not "hunched-up," or over, and in a straight-horizontal line.

Breath is continuously relaxed and steady without holding your breath during movements.

No tension is used in body, mind, or spirit, to execute relaxed feminine movements in this dance.

Stay relaxed during all movements, always.

Never hold on to the body while executing Egyptian dance.

The stomach and derriere are relaxed.

HEALTH BENEFITS:

Body parts strengthened:

Good posture adds to overall health and wellness.

Good posture increases good physical circulation and assimilation of vital organs and helps in coordination and balance and gives overall feelings of wellness.

'HIP WORKS'

HIP DROPS

"Construct a Mind Palace"

"How to Change Your Life Calendar"

Stand in basic structure and position.

On the downbeat of music, with all weight under right foot, move right knee slightly back as you slightly lift side of right hip.

Complete move by immediately stretching and extending same right hip slightly downwards, slightly past waistline, as you slightly bend right knee.

Repeat on the other side.

HEALTH BENEFITS:

Body parts strengthened:

Bladder, rectum, female organs, sigmoid colon

HIP SLIDES

"Everybody is a Star. Doesn't matter who You are!"

Sly Stone

Stand in basic structure and position.

Feet flat.

Weight evenly distributed under feet.

Keep both knees straight, not tight.

Upper torso must be held in a consistent lifted position and kept still/silent for entire duration of movement.

Move hips <u>slightly</u> from side-to-side, slightly right, and back to center, and slightly left, and back to center.

When shifting weight to left, all weight is under ball & heel of flat left foot, and vice versa.

NOTE:

Motion comes from the pelvis and hips area.

Stretch and extend sides of each hip right, and back to center, and repeating left in order to draw maximum horizontal line with hips as you shift weight from one side to the other still keeping torso in a lifted position in order to isolate torso from the hip area.

Remember to keep rib cage lifted to get maximum horizontal movements and lines in hips/pelvis.

12

HIP SLIDES

(*continued*)

HEALTH BENEFITS:

Body parts strengthened:

Bladder, rectum, female organs, sigmoid colon

A clear path to moving better begins with the hips.

HIP LIFTS

"I Am / You Are 20 Feet tall."

Erykah Badu

Stand in basic structure and position.

Place all weight equally under both flat feet.

Both knees are slightly bent.

At hip level, on the downbeat of music, move right knee slightly backwards as you lift side of left hip, at 9 o'clock, slightly upwards for two or four counts, then move same hip back to starting position.

Repeat on other side at 3 o'clock position, or right hip-side.

NOTE: Keep feet flat.

Do not lift heels or feet.

Stretch and extend hip while lifting only the hip slightly upwards.

Do not lean left or right.

Keep body in upright position during hip lifts to better isolate moving hips only. Please don't tilt body during this movement.

HEALTH BENEFITS:

Body parts strengthened:

Bladder, rectum, female organs, sigmoid colon.

A clear path to moving better begins with the hips.

HIP CIRCLES

"Your mind is in divine order.
Your body is in divine order. You are in divine order."

Barrie Konicov

Imagine a small circle that's flat on the floor.

Stand inside circle with feet hip-width apart.

Place both feet on both outer sides of small circle.

The left foot is on the left side of the circle, or 9 o'clock, and the right foot is on the right side of the circle, or 3 o'clock.

With bottom-center of pelvis as a drawing device, (not sides of hips) imagine numbers of a small clock, flat on the floor between your feet, where you're drawing small circles with the bottom, or at 6 o'clock at the bottom-center of your pelvis.

Lift pelvic bone very slightly in front/center to 12 o'clock position.

Repeat same movement, as just stated above, lifting at 3 o'clock, lifting at 6 o'clock, 9 o'clock, and back up to 12 o'clock.

Reverse movement back from 12 o'clock, to 11 o'clock, 9 o'clock, 6 o'clock, up to 3 o'clock, and finally to 12 o'clock.

Now repeat all same movements with one smooth clockwise circle from 12-to-12, then "draw" one smooth counterclockwise circle from 12-12 while keeping the pelvic bone or pelvis lifted as you draw hip circle "around-the-clock."

HIP CIRCLES

(*continued*)

HEALTH BENEFITS

Body parts strengthened:

Brainstem, female organs, rectum, sigmoid colon

Hip movements bring vitality, happy feelings, massage spinal cord, gives a clear path to moving better, and improves the quality of life.

"FERRIS WHEEL" HIP CIRLCE

ACCENTED/MOVING DOWNWARD

"Spiritual breakthrough speeded by deliberate dispossession."
"Less is More. The art of voluntary poverty"

By VandenBroeck

Stand in basic structure and position.

Must keep upper body lifted during entire movement.

Imagine a very-small Ferris-Wheel-like circle that's placed in a straight line, not a flat circle, like a clock, at hip level, centered and in front of you. Once again, at hip level, imagine a circle in center-front of hips in a "Ferris Wheel" circle, not in a flat circle.

Place pelvic bone in a pelvic lift/tilt, which should start with a lifted-upward position. Breathe naturally.

Lift pelvis to top of small Ferris wheel, which is the 12 o'clock position.

Stretch, extend, and move pelvis slightly forward and moving downward to the 3 o'clock position of Ferris Wheel.

As you keep the stretch and extension of pelvis, keep moving pelvis down through 4, 5, and to the 6 o'clock position.

"Ferris Wheel" Hip Circle

(*continued*)

Once at 6 o'clock position, move pelvis slightly back, tilt pelvis up, hold tilt, breathe naturally, while drawing pelvic circle smoothly back up while "drawing" a half circle up through, 7, 8, 9, 10, 11, to

12 o'clock position, and repeat.

NOTE: Twelve o'clock position, at this point, is in front of you in an upward position.

HEALTH BENEFITS:

Body parts strengthened:

Brain stem, female organs, rectum, sigmoid colon.

Hip moves, clears, and purges negative energy, in root chakra.

Hip movements, bring vitality, happy feelings, massages the spinal cord, gives a clear path to moving better, and improves

quality of life.

PELVIC HIP CIRCLE

The more we love, the less we have to think.

"Loving Yourself"

Lawrence Crane

Stand in basic structure and position.

At the bottom-center of your pelvic bone, imagine drawing and outlining a circle between your feet.

The circle is flat on the floor.

Lift pelvic bone slightly up and forward for one count.

Release pelvic bone to natural position; stretch and extend while slightly lifting right side of hip up just past waist level for one count.

Lift tail bone slightly up for one count.

Stretch and extend while slightly lifting left side of hip up just past the waist level for one count.

Complete hip circle by lifting pelvic bone slightly up, again, for one count.

REVERSE MOVEMENTS

COUNTERCLOCKWISE

Now, execute all moves using the points stated above while drawing smooth and continuous flat-small hip circles, for four counts continuously left and/or four counts continuously right, or clockwise.

Repeat and Practice

Pelvic Hip Circle

(*continued*)

HEALTH BENEFITS:

Body parts strengthened:

Brain, brainstem, pancreas, stomach, kidney, liver bladder, female organs, sigmoid colon, rectum

Hip moves alleviates, pain and irritation, and is a clear path to moving better and improves quality of life.

PELVIC WAVE

"It takes just a little extra effort to be above average."

"Success Gems"

Jewel Diamond Taylor

Stand in basic structure and position.

Isolate all body parts only using the pelvic area.

Move tail bone slightly back-and-up.

Hold tail bone in this back-and-up position for two counts.

Move lifted tail bone slightly forward for two counts.

Contract and release while lifting pelvic bone as you move pelvis slightly backward for two counts with a goal of moving slight forward and backward while presenting a wave-like effect.

Repeat

HEALTH BENEFITS:

Body parts strengthened:

Bladder, female organs, and sigmoid colon

FIGURE 8s (Infinities)

Movement accented Backward.

"Be yourself but be your best self!"

Khalidah Kali

Stand in basic structure and position.

Keep upper body lifted, breathe evenly.

Keep hips "squared," and straight forward in natural position, not tilted, forward or backward.

How to outline a horizontal Figure 8 moving backward with hips, parallel to the floor:

Imagine a large clock on the floor in which you stand in the center of it.

Place all weight under flat right foot as you slightly stretch and extend right hip to 1 o'clock, keeping hip extended to the right while moving in half circle downward, stretching and extending hip, drawing a half circle to the 5 o'clock.

At above 5 o'clock, shift weight to left flat foot (without leaning left), keep right foot flat under slightly bent knee, as you stretch and extend left hip upward and across to 11 o'clock, then stretching and extending hip circularly down to 7 o'clock.

Repeat

In other words, you're moving the hips from 1 o'clock, to 5 o'clock, crossing up to 11 o'clock, and down to 7 o'clock, and repeating.

Figure 8s – Infinities

(*continued*)

Remember:

Stretch and extend hips from side-to-side. Keep torso lifted during entire movement to isolate and move the pelvic/hip area only.

Don't hold your breath.

Isolate meaning, absolutely no other part of body moves during this particular hip movement.

PLEASE NOTE:

One complete Hip Figure 8 consists of four hip positions to complete only one smooth-and-continuous Figure 8 movement of the hips.

HEALTH BENEFITS:

Body parts strengthened:

Brain, brainstem, bladder, rectum, female organs, sigmoid colon

A clear path to moving better begins with the hips and improves quality of life.

HIP SHIMMY/QUIVER

Any situation is transformed into perfection when you apply love.

"Loving Yourself"

Lawrence Crane

This movement is great for womb wellness, relieves tension, and so much fun to do!

Everybody loves this popular hip movement!

Have fun!

Stand in basic structure and position.

It's important to place weight evenly under both feet, under the balls and heels of both feet in making yourself grounded.

Keep knees slightly bent, making sure that knee movements are going back-and-forth meaning, when one knee is slightly forward, the other knee is slightly back.

Never stretch knee all the way back.

Once you bend your knees slightly, stay at that position while not moving knees up and down during movement.

Always keep knees moving in forward/back motions for hip quiver.

TO DO HIP QUIVER:

While keeping both knees bent, subtly move left knee forward, while right knee moves subtly back.

Keep alternating this forward/back movement slowly, then build speed with forward/back knee movement while keeping moves

Hip Shimmy/Quiver
(*continued*)

shallow and slight to cause flesh on thighs and hips to
"shake" continuously.

Must keep hips loose and relaxed to do movement successfully.

PRACTICE AND REPEAT

HEALTH BENEFITS:

Body Parts Strengthened:

Female organs, rectum, sigmoid colon

Hip movements are a pathway to better balance, strength in hips, and walking.

LAYERING HIP MOVEMENTS

(MOVEMENTS COMBINED)

PELVIC ARCH AND CONTRACTION (RELEASE) COMBINED WITH QUIVERING/SHAKING

I love you. Sorry. Please forgive me. Thank You!"
Saidia Therapy Lady, Chicago

Stand in basic structure and position.

Contract; lifting pelvis up and forward.

Lift tail bone up (behind you) as if you are going to "sit down."

Alternate pubic bone and tail bone movements by lifting pubic bone up (in front of you,) then moving tail bone up behind you.)

All following movements are done all at-same-time:

Keep all weight mostly under flat feet of both heels, and the rest of weight under balls of feet, while keeping all toes flat and grounded, while hips are alternating movement with fast-shallow up-and-down motions from sides of both hips with slightly bent knees for entire movement.

The fast-shallow up-and-down motions create a quivering affect.

Hips must remain loose, relaxed, and not tense.

PLEASE NOTE: When one knee is slightly forward, the other knee is slightly back.

Do not bounce during any moves.

Hips move up and down, not knees.

PELVIC ARCH AND CONTRACTION (RELEASE) COMBINED WITH QUIVERING/SHAKING
(*continued*)

HEALTH BENEFITS:

Body parts strengthened:

Brain, brain stem, bladder, rectum, female organs, sigmoid colon

Hip moves clear and purges negative energy in root chakra.

Hip movements bring vitality & happy feelings, massage the spinal cord, gives a clear path to moving better, and improves quality of life.

HIP SHIMMY/QUIVERING WALK

Drink half your weight in ounces of water daily.

Stand in basic structure and position.

In one spot, place all weight under ball and heel of both feet.

Keep both knees bent slightly throughout the entire movement.

Start moving right knee slightly forward as left knee moves slightly backwards.

Pick up the speed of knees moving slightly forward and backward and keep muscles on hips relaxed until you see and feel a quivering of the thighs and hips while keeping both feet flat with all weight under ball and heel of both flat feet.

Do not bounce. Hips go up and down, not knees.

NOTE:

When moving knees forward and back, the hips on both sides are moving slightly up and down.

An example of this is when the left knee moves slightly forward, the right hip moves slightly up, and when the right knee is slightly forward, the left hip moves slightly up, to travel, walk with quivering movement.

PELVIC ARCH AND CONTRACTION (RELEASE)
COMBINED WITH QUIVERING/SHAKING
HIP SHIMMY/QUIVER WALK
(*continued*)

Keep all weight on forward foot while maintaining quiver as stated above, not stopping quiver while transiting/brushing back foot to forward position and repeat the hip quivering walk.

Repeat and Practice

HEALTH BENEFITS:

Body parts strengthened:

Bladder, female organs, sigmoid colon

"CHOO-CHOO" TRAIN SHIMMY/WALK
("A KISS IS NOT A PROMISE")

Stand in basic structure and position.

Take short-fast, right and left flat-footed steps while traveling forward on slightly bended knees. Weight on balls of flat feet.

Please don't lift knees up-and-down, that would make the movement jerky and bouncy, which is what we do not want.

While keeping both knees on the same levels, not letting knees go up and down, do this movement:

As you loosen and soften the flesh on thighs and hips, keep quivering affect with shallow up and down motions on both sides of hips and thighs (without raising knees up and down,) as you step like a "shuffle" with feet, with very small and shallow up & down motions on both sides of hips while maintaining the quivering effect for the "Choo-Choo Train Shimmy."

NOTE: The sides of hips are moving, very subtly, and quickly up-and down, not the knees.

Once you move one foot forward, don't move that foot

immediately back. Keep traveling progressively forward.

"CHOO-CHOO" TRAIN SHIMMY

(*continued*)

Move one foot quickly forward, then move other foot quickly forward. Repeat. Practice.

HEALTH BENEFITS:

Body parts strengthened:

Female organs, rectum, sigmoid colon.

Hip movements bring vitality and happy feelings,

massage spinal cord, gives a clear path to moving better,

and improves quality of life.

PELVIC WAVE WITH QUIVERING EFFECT

"True affluence is not needing anything."

"Less is more. The art of voluntary poverty"

Goldian VandenBroeck

Stand in basic structure and position.

Execute all instructions and "Pelvic Wave," as previously written.

To combine "quivering effect," execute and maintain Pelvic Wave as you execute rapid, tiny, alternating forward and backward knee movements, while keeping both knees slightly bent, while moving knees backward and forward, alternating knees, while keeping weight heavy under ball-and-heel of both flat feet.

NOTE: While one knee is slightly forward, the other knee is slightly back.

HEALTH BENEFITS:

Body parts strengthened:

Bladder, female organs, sigmoid colon, brain, brainstem

FIGURE 8 WITH QUIVERING EFFECT

"To have what we want is riches, but to be able to do without is power!"

"Less is more. The art of voluntary poverty."

Goldian VandenBroeck

Stand in basic structure and position.

Execute all instructions in "Figure 8 (Infinities)" as previously written.

During the same time that you perform the figure 8 with the hips, execute rapid, tiny, alternating knee movements with both knees slightly bent, while moving knees slightly and rapidly backward and forward with heavy weight under ball-and-heel of both flat feet.

NOTE: While one knee is slightly forward, the other knee is slightly backward.

Repeat and Practice.

HEALTH BENEFITS:

Body parts strengthened:

Pancreas, stomach, kidney, liver, bladder, female organs, sigmoid colon, rectum

HIP QUIVER/SHIMMY
WITH HIP SLIDES

"Do your best, and let God do the rest."

Execute entire instructions in Hip Slides as you slightly quiver hips keeping flesh of glutes and derriere, loose, relaxed, and softened to execute the quivering motion in hips.

NOTE:

To quiver on the hips, use a very-slight and very fast alternating forward-and-back movement of the knees as you keep knees almost straight but not tight/tense.

Keep rib cage lifted to isolate torso from hips area.

IMPORTANT:

The upper body of torso is lifted and not moving, at all, for

the entire duration of this movement.

Hands are 'silent,' and shouldn't shake during movement.

To prevent movement of hands during the above movement, totally relax hands with no tension, and hold both arms down with both hands slightly behind hips, with elbows and wrists still.

Elbows are not very stiff yet are still. Your fingers are relaxed.

Practice! Practice! Practice! Have fun!

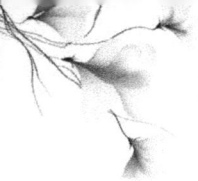

HIP QUIVER/SHIMMY WITH HIP SLIDES

(*continued*)

HEALTH BENEFITS:

Body parts strengthened:

Bladder, rectum, female organs, sigmoid colon

A clear path to moving better, begins with the hips,

and improves the quality of life.

PELVIC CIRCLES WITH QUIVERING HIPS

"Everybody is a star. Everybody wants to shine."

Sly Stone

Stand in basic structure and position.

Imagine a flat-small circle between your feet using bottom-center of pelvis as an imaginary drawing devise.

While drawing circle in a four-count, continuously smooth, clockwise circle, repeating the four counts counterclockwise,

layer entire move with a quivering hip.

Layering means you are quivering hips at the same time

you are executing the hip circle.

Quiver hips as you draw circle with hips by moving both knees rapidly with shallow moves forward and backward.

When one knee is back, the other knee forward.

Knees never move all the way back.

Additionally, to quiver hips, both hips alternate with shallow

up-and-down moves from sides of hips.

HEALTH BENEFITS:

Body parts strengthened:

Brain, brain stem, bladder, rectum, female organs, sigmoid colon

PELVIC CIRCLES WITH QUIVERING HIPS

(*continued*)

Hip moves clears, and purges, negative energy in root chakra.

Hip movements, bring vitality, happy feelings, massage spinal cord, gives clear path to moving better, and improves quality of life.

HIP CIRCLES WITH QUIVER

"Be and stay at your highest level of self-value
and self-worth."

By Iyanla Vanzant

Maintain all movements as in *Hip Circle Chapter*

As you maintain the hip circle movement, drop sides of both hips, alternatively, in shallow upward-and-downward, quick motions, so fast, that the flesh of the thighs and hips move loosely and relaxed and move like jelly.

Repeat

HEALTH BENEFITS:

Body Parts Strengthened:

Female organs, colon, rectum, sigmoid colon

Clears root chakra.

CHEST MOVEMENTS

CHEST SLIDES

"Be blessed and be a blessing!"

Stand in basic structure and position.

Place weight altogether under heels, pads/balls of flat feet.

Bend knees very slightly.

(Important) Slightly stretch torso upward while lifting/isolating chest from lower torso.

Do not hold your breath.

Hold above position as you stretch.

Slide and extend your chest a few inches left-of-center, move torso back to center and repeat right-of-center.

Move chest back to center.

Repeat.

HEALTH BENEFITS:

Body parts strengthened:

Heart, chest, and thoracic cavity

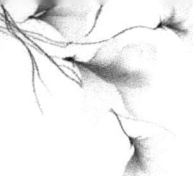

CHEST QUIVER

"Pretty is not an accomplishment. Beauty is a spirit."

Khalidah Kali

Stand in basic structure and position.

Use gentle/subtle forward & back shallow-shoulder movements, meaning one shoulder is forward as the other shoulder is back.

Alternate the movements, making shoulders quickly rock gently forward and backward to allow the breast to move gently like jelly.

Movements must be kept gentle, not hard.

HEALTH BENEFITS:

Body parts strengthened:

Brain, brainstem, breast, chest, and thoracic cavity.

CHEST WAVES

"Everybody is a star. It doesn't matter who you are."

Sly Stone

Stand in basic structure and position.

Imagine a small perpendicular "Ferris Wheel" circle at chest level and follow that circle with your chest.

Arch and lift back slowly up to 12 o'clock in the "wheel," moving slightly forward, and forming a half circle.

Slowly, move chest slightly down to 3 o'clock, which is at a natural/neutral chest position.

Slowly, gently, slightly, and subtly round back to

"bottom-of-wheel" to 6 o'clock.

Start slowly arching back up to half circle to the

12 o'clock position, and repeat.

CHEST WAVES

(*continued*)

HEALTH BENEFITS:

Body parts strengthened:

Heart, heart chakra, and thoracic cavity; feelings of peace

CHEST LIFTS/DROPS

"Minimize Consumption. Maximize Wellness"

(Quote By Ghandhi)

"Art of Voluntary Poverty"

Goldian VandenBroeck

Stand in basic structure and position.

Place chest centered and straight-forward, not lifted or dropped from the center.

Inhale as you gently, and subtly squeeze shoulder blades (the scapulars), located behind your back, which subtly give a shallow lift of the chest. Hold two counts.

Exhale as you open scapulars to natural position as chest naturally returns to centered natural position, not lifted or below center level of torso.

Repeat

Aim for soft and gentle texture in this movement with a very shallow lifting and back to center-starting position.

HEALTH BENEFITS:

Body parts strengthened:

Breast and thoracic cavity; spinal massage
Clears, cleans, and purges heart chakra

LAYERING CHEST MOVEMENTS

(Movements Combined)

TORSO UNDULATIONS (WAVES)

"Love is its own reward."

"Loving Yourself"

Lawrence Crane

PLEASE NOTE: Four bodily positions are engaged all at the same time during this forward-swaying as well as backward-swaying movements as follows:

Stand in basic structure and position.

1. Both knees slightly bent.

The right foot is placed slightly forward on flat foot with all weight under right foot, ball and heel.

The left flat foot is back with no weight on left flat foot.

2. Knees straight, not tight or stiff.

3. Tail bone lifted and at-same-time, chest is lifted to cause an arch in back.

1 through 3 are engaged all at-the-same time as you move slightly forward.

TORSO UNDULATIONS (WAVES)

(*continued*)

TRANSITION FROM FORWARD TO BACKWARD MOVEMENT:

1. Shift weight to left-back foot.
2. All weight is under ball and heel of left-back flat foot.
3. Bending both knees slightly.
4. Contract/lift pelvic bone slightly.
5. While bringing chest from arched/lifted position to neutral.

REPEAT & PRACTICE

NOTE: 1 through 5 are engaged, all at-same-time as you move slightly backward.

HEALTH BENEFITS:

Body parts strengthened:

Nervous system and spine

Sculpts, tones, and firms abdominals.

Digestion

CHEST SLIDE WITH CHEST QUIVER

"Do your best, and let God do the rest!"

Stand in basic structure and position.

While executing chest slide as described previously, keep torso lifted with relaxed breast area, softened and quivering (slightly shaking.)

In fast motion, while one shoulder is slightly forward, the other shoulder is slightly back, essentially moving shoulders quickly forward and back with the chest area moving slightly from side-to-side.

HEALTH BENEFITS:

Body parts strengthened:

Heart, chest, thoracic cavity

LAYERING SHOULDERS, ARMS, AND HANDS

(Movements Combined)

BREAST AND SHOULDER SHIMMY

"Love is the means and the end."

"Loving Yourself "

Lawrence Crane

Stand in basic structure and position.

Move each shoulder, accenting forward only slightly while alternating each shoulder, meaning, while the right shoulder is slightly forward, the left shoulder is slightly back; then the left shoulder comes forward while the right shoulder goes back, and repeat.

This movement is moving, "double-time," and until flesh on breasts are moving only slightly like jelly.

This movement is done very gently and subtly,

Never with a hard shake!

REPEAT

HEALTH BENEFITS:

Body parts strengthened:

Brain, brainstem, breast, thoracic cavity; calming

CONTINUOUS, ALTERNATING BACKWARD AND FORWARD MOVING SHOULDER CIRCLES

(S)he who knows (s)he has enough, is rich!

"Less is more. The art of voluntary poverty."

Goldian VandenBroeck

Stand in basic structure and position.

See/feel imaginary small-flat circle on side of upper-relaxed

left or right shoulder.

Move side of either upper shoulder slightly forward, for one count; slightly up, for one count; slightly back, for one count; and slightly back down to your original position.

Alternate, and execute same movement on other shoulder.

REPEAT

NOTE: Make smooth, continuous, non-stop-small shoulder circles using the four directions mentioned above, forward, up, back, and down. Repeat.

Each movement is very slight as you draw the continuous shoulder move.

TO MOVE SHOULDERS TO FORWARD CIRCLES:

Simply change the circle directions as described above.

Move shoulders back, up, forward, and down, reversing above direction of backward shoulder moves.

CONTINUOUS ALTERNATING BACKWARD AND FORWARD MOVING SHOULDER CIRCLES

(*continued*)

HEALTH BENEFITS:

Body parts strengthened:

Brain, brainstem, heart, breast, thoracic cavity,

DOUBLE HORIZONTAL ARMS & HANDS WAVE WITH SHOULDERS MOVING BACKWARD

(Horizontal Arm Waves)

"Spiritual breakthrough speeded by deliberate dispossession!"

"Less is more. The art of voluntary poverty."

Goldian VandenBroeck

Stand in basic structure and position.

Imagine a large clock before you.

Place both arms in a horizontal line, where the left hand is at 9 o'clock position, and the right hand is at the 3 o'clock position.

Both shoulders are relaxed in a natural position, and the body is totally squared, and facing forward.

The side of the left shoulder is at 9 o'clock, and the side of the right shoulder is at 3 o'clock.

Elbows are kept almost straight yet relaxed during movement.

Keep both palms facing down.

All the following movements are performed at the same time:

The side of right shoulder slightly lifts and moves slightly back in a circular movement.

DOUBLE HORIZONTAL ARMS & HANDS WAVE
WITH SHOULDERS MOVING BACKWARD
Horizontal Hand Wave
(*continued*)

Still keeping arms placed horizontally, repeat same movement on the left shoulder.

As right elbow comes slightly up and down, repeat on left elbow moving up and then down, as left wrist and hand moves up and down, right wrist and hand moves up and down.

NOTE: You are still outlining small circles on the sides of both shoulders, moving, forward, up, back, and down, alternating, during this entire movement.

Practice & Repeat

HEALTH BENEFITS:

Body parts strengthened:

Heart, lungs

SOFT HAND WAVE

SOFT HAND WAVE

"Be blessed and be a blessing."

Stand in basic structure and position.

This hand movement uses wrists, palms, and fingers, only.

Lift right forearm and hand straight up.

Arch palm of hand; meaning you are pushing an arch in middle of hand with lifted, straight, spread-tense fingers and thumb while keeping arched position.

Move your hand and fingers downward for four counts while keeping arched position.

Fingers are stretched out during a smooth four-count downward move.

Relax fingers and hand totally after hand is in downward position.

Lift hand and fingers up in four continuous smooth counts, keeping hand and fingers relaxed and faced downward during the upward movement with the wrist.

Once the wrist is in total upward position, slowly lift softened fingers to 12o'clock position, and repeat.

HEALTH BENEFITS:

A very relaxing effect.

Helps relieve repetitive-movement syndromes.

57

SOFT HAND WAVE

(*continued*)

Sculpts, tones upper and lower arms when executing movements with arm and hands in upward positions.

Promotes tranquility.

Effective in acquiring muscle mass in upper arm.

NECK SLIDES

A very "flirty and exotic" isolated head move where the head is "floating" over the neck!

Stand in basic structure and position.

Imagine a clock in front of you.

While keeping your nose and mouth forward and centered, keeping chin parallel to the floor, stretch and extend your head while moving your left ear slightly to the left at 9 o'clock without tilting your head up, or down, or lifting your chin up, or down.

Hold position to the left for two counts, then stretch and extend, while moving, and isolating your head to the initial center again.

NECK SLIDES

(*continued*)

Repeat above instructions, while stretching and extending the head slightly to the right or 3 o'clock position, holding that position for two counts, and back to the initial center.

Alternating Neck Slide:

Continuously move your head in a very small, subtle way, back-and-forth horizontally (without hesitation through the center,) between 9 o'clock and 3 o'clock while making smooth movements.

Enjoy!

HEALTH BENEFITS:

Body parts strengthened:

— The Medulla Oblongata —

(The connection between brain and spinal cord connecting

heart, respiratory, nerves and spinal cord.)

So refreshing to the Spirit!

So visually beautiful and pretty!

4 EGYPTIAN DANCE

COMBINATIONS

The following are Egyptian dance combinations of single dance movements previously described.

All combinations flow continuously from one movement to the next, without hesitation, except where stated.

If any concerns regarding how to execute any movements within the dance combinations, simply refer to movements previously described for details, or purchase my instructional dance DVDs, hardcopy or virtually, or email your question to me. khalidah@att.net

Thank you for your patience and understanding.

Also, please see "Books and Resources" page, toward back of book, for further information, and to make purchases.

#1 EGYPTIAN DANCE COMBINATION

Key: L-Left. R-Right

1. 2 Torso Waves, 2 counts each,

2L & 2R

2. Step-Turn to R in 2 counts

Ending moves facing forward.

(Do a 1-Count pause)

3. Downward-accented hip figure 8,

horizontally, parallel to wall in front

of you for four counts

NOTE: When using music, speed of movement

must be consistent with the speed of music.

REPEAT

Start #1 to the Right.

NOTE: There are 11 counts of movement in the above

combination.

E N J O Y

#2 EGYPTIAN DANCE COMBINATION

1. Hand waves; 2 L & 2 R, while using both hands, left and right

2. 2 hip drops L – 2 hip drops R

3. Full-Body "Shimmy/Quiver" for 8 counts as each arm goes up both sides of body, at same time, with "Shimmy/Quiver"

REPEAT

#3 EGYPTIAN DANCE COMBINATION

As seen Live, on-location, in Egypt,

Performed by Soheir Zaki,

(A Very Great Egyptian Dance Icon/Queen.)

1. Slow/small R-hip circles for three slow counts as you turn with right-shoulder moving back.

2. On 4th count, as you face forward,

perform 2 torso waves; 2L & 2R

3. 2 hip drops left; 2 hip drops right

REPEAT

#4 EGYPTIAN DANCE COMBINATION

1. Hip figure 8s parallel to the floor.

4 hip fig. 8s L / Repeat R

2. Torso waves, 2L & 2R

3. 4-count stationary hip quiver

4. 2-count turn (L or R) ending front

5. 1-count pause

6. 4-count arm waves – L, Repeat R

REPEAT

FINGER CYMBALS

FINGER CYMBALS

In Egypt, and Arabic, it's called, Sagat, and in Turkey, Istanbul, it's called Zills.

It's played with a set-of-four cymbals on thumbs and middle fingers.

Brass cymbals give the best sound.

It's best to start with the smaller ones, two inches in diameter, which are lighter, and easier to use.

Larger cymbals give louder sound when playing for outdoors, large rooms, and for more advanced/skilled dancers.

Use cymbals with two parallel slots for elastic.

Flat strips of elastic ("braid elastic") are better than round ones.

Cheaper cymbals have one hole, and are hard to play, and the sound is not good.

Thread elastic from bottom of cymbals to the top of cymbals. Place fingers between both sides of the elastic to adjust elastic length on both sides of fingers. Fasten with a small safety pin on top of cymbals. Elastic must be snug on fingers, or almost tight, or the tonal quality will not be good.

Place cymbals on thumbs and middle fingers immediately below bottom of nail bed and right above top of first joint of each thumb and middle fingers with palms facing upward, and the inside of cymbals facing up, too.

Deliberately lift-and-bend top joint of middle finger cymbals up to the thumb cymbals while the thumb cymbal is extended with a straight-thumb-joint, to 3 o'clock on the right hand, and with a straight-thumb-joint extended to 9 o'clock on the left hand while deliberately striking with lower middle fingers, up, quickly and lightly, to the thumbs.

NOTE: The thumbs move automatically "on-their-own." Just focus on bringing middle fingers up to touch thumb cymbals.

Before playing cymbals, but with cymbals on fingers, keep hands relaxed with top and bottom cymbals close together, without cymbals touching.

Palms are held up with arms opened wide like a medium-sized beach ball at chest level.

Key: R = Right Hand /   L= Left Hand

Basic/Standard Finger Cymbal Beats:

Single Time: Touch with both cymbals together, at same time, on right side Only.

Repeat left and right again, as follows:

R Hand- One second pause

L Hand – One second pause

R Hand – One second pause

Meaning touching both cymbals on the right side together, at the same time, then lift them away from each other, a little bit, then repeat on the left side.

Slowly, touch cymbals together as described above. Using "Single Time."

Single time: 'RL RL 'RL 'RL

Double time: 'RLR 'RLR 'RLR

(Single hyphen means accent on that R)

There are very, many basic rhythms played across north Africa, and the Middle East.

We're exploring only two popular rhythms, or popular patterns that are played with cymbals.

Creativity of musical patterns played with finger cymbals consistent-to-music can go into infinity.

BALEDI RHYTHM   (Folkloric)

'RR RLR 'R RLR

CHIFTI TELLI RHYTHM (Contemporary)

(Chifti Telli is a Turkish word and rhythm)

(Single time) 'R'R 'RLRL 'RR 'L

There's so much more detail regarding use of finger cymbals in my "Finger Cymbals," DVD that can be purchased hard copy or virtually through my website, khalidahsdance.com or by contacting me through my email, khalidah@att.net

The focus is to play cymbals with the beat-of-the-music.

Please see "Books Resources" page.

HEALTH BENEFITS:

Body Parts Strengthened: Hands, Wrists, Arms

Relieves carpal tunnel, a repetitive movement syndrome. Sculpts, tones, and firms arms.

V E I L S # 1 of 2

("L" SHAPED-TURN)

**"God is in the blessings business,
and I am in business with God!"**

A DANCE FAVORITE!

VEILS =DANCING WITH FLOWING FABRICS!

TWO VEIL DANCE PATTERNS: (1 of 2)

Stand in basic structure and position.

Imagine a very large clock in front of you.

Stand forward with right arm straight up to ceiling,

at 12 o'clock, or top center.

The left arm is held horizontally left to the 9 o'clock position.

Hold the upper arm and the horizontal arm in above positions, while keeping the elbows straight, while moving in following directions.

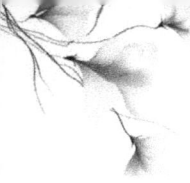

V E I L S #1 of 2

"L" SHAPED-TURN

(*continued*)

Move with a right-shoulder-back turn while moving with the right foot, then left foot, then right foot, and then left foot again, while moving in a small circle, which takes you back to the starting position.

Repeat left, starting with left foot, right, left, and right while moving, again, in a small circle in smooth continuous moves without stopping at each step. You are moving in a continuous turn.

Repeat and alternate

HEALTH BENEFITS:

Body parts strengthened:

Sculpts, tones, and firm arms; heart health, coordination

Color therapy is applied with veils.

For example:

Purple = Royalty, majesty, magic, mystery

Blue   = Serenity, peacefulness, clarity

      Et cetera

NOTE: When using Veils, you are receiving physical, color, and sound therapy, all at the same time!

VEILS # 2 of 2

FIGURE 8 VEILS
WITH COMBINATIONS

"SEE IT TO SEE IT!"

"SEEK IT TO SEE IT!"

Stand in basic structure and position.

The intention of a "Figure 8 Veil" is to draw a very large

figure 8, with flowing fabric, in front of you while receiving

multiples of therapy. Eight is a number of stability!

Imagine a very large clock in front of you.

Place your left hand at center-back of your waistline with left elbow horizontally left at the 9 o'clock position behind you while holding, at least, 3 ½ yards of silk, chiffon, or other soft fabric in your left hand with index and third fingers on top of fabric and thumb underneath fabric. Hold fabric firmly enough so as not to let fabric fall out of your hand. Holding does Not have to be tight.

You are holding upper-left corner of fabric in your left hand

behind your back.

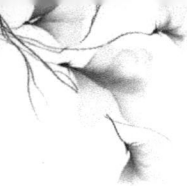

VEILS # 2 OF 2

(Part 2 of 2 – Continued)

NOTE: Before putting left hand behind back, place both arms across relaxed shoulders in horizontal line while holding fabric with remainder of fabric flowing downward, equally on each side of body, like curtains on a window with slight dip in fabric at top-center of "window." Place fabric Behind you.

Now, keep left hand at center-back of waistline.

Hold the upper-right hand corner of fabric with your right hand; your "free" hand to draw with. (Your right hand)

If over 5' 5," please use four yards of fabric.

Once again, keep your left elbow at 9 o'clock with left hand behind your center-back as you draw with Right hand on right side of your body, starting with right hand and arm down by your side.

Draw a large, almost swift, not jerky, half circle up to 12 o'clock around to 9 o'clock down and across to 5 o'clock, half circle up to 9 o'clock, while continuing to outline a large 8.

Your left-hand stays center-back of your waistline while holding the upper left-top corner with the left hand, as you are drawing with the right hand and arm.

Repeat to draw with left arm and hand while placing right hand center-back of waistline with elbow facing the 3 o'clock position.

Keep practicing in a mirror until you see yourself using large, continuous sweeping motions to outline the figure 8 on left and right.

VEILS # 2 OF 2

(*Part 2 of 2 – continued*)

Keep movement of fabric smooth.

The "sweeping" fabric should go above your head with a straight elbow while keeping the elbow straight for the entire draw.

It is very important to draw this large figure 8, without hesitation,

in one big continuous movement.

Keeping elbow straight while, drawing the 8 is very important.

BEAUTIFUL SIMPLE VEIL COMBINATIONS

Let's make very beautiful veil combinations by combining the

"L" & "8" Veils!

AFTER drawing veil in the Figure 8, place arms in the L-shape.

Keep arms in L shape while making a four-count, right-shoulder-back turn, to the right.

Repeat left, while making a very pretty combination of the

"L" and "8" veil patterns.

E N J O Y!!

PICTURES

Khalidah Kali at Taj Mahal in Agra, India

LEFT-TO-RIGHT
TIPSUDAH, FOLASHADE, KHALIDAH (CENTER)
MARIA-ADIA, CHACHANA
**Khalidah's North African Dance Experience, Inc.,
at Field Museum, Chicago, Performing at Cleopatra Exhibit**

*Exquisite Egyptian 'Belly' Dance Moves, Fun*Fitness*Femininity*

LEFT-TO-RIGHT
FOLASHADE, LINDA, KHALIDAH (CENTER)
ALESIA , CHACHANA
TOP-CENTER, TORRENCE
Khalidah's North African Dance Experience, Inc.
Performing at Cantigny Park, Wheaton, Illinois' African Festival

Khalidah Instructing in Las Vagas, Nevada

Khalidah in Performance in California

at Rakkasah Dance Festival

HEALTHY FOODS, INGREDIENTS, AND NUTRITIONAL VALUES

Included in this chapter are food suggestions for better health, wellness, and quality of life using healthy food ingredients, in pictures, and exploring details of nutritional values.

All foods & photographs in this chapter, prepared by Khalidah Kali.

— Photo: Raw Green Leaf Salad

— Photo: Sautéed Green Vegetables in Water

— Photo: Green Drink

— Photo: Fruit Drink (Smoothie)

— Photo: Jasmine Green Tea

— Photo: Hibiscus Tea

NOTE: Consult your professional medical physician, before consuming new foods, and exercises.

RAW GREEN LEAF SALAD

Raw Green Leaf Salad

Vitamin K, helps build bones, strengthens vision, improves hydration, bone maintenance, potassium, magnesium, strengthens heartbeats.

—RED ONION—

Anti-inflammatory, reduces cholesterol, protects against blood clots, reduces blood pressure

—CUCUMBER—

Vitamin C, vitamin K, vitamin A, antioxidant, hydration,

promotes regularity

—TOMATO—

Reduces risk of heart disease, cancer, great source of vitamin C, vitamin K

—AVOCADO—

Protects the eyes, vitamin C, vitamin K, vitamin D, reduces

blood cholesterol

—SCALLIONS

Strengthens eyes and vision.

SAUTÉED GREEN VEGETABLES IN WATER

(Sauteed Green Vegetables in Water)

SPINACH

— Helps to prevent heart disease

— Helps to prevent cancer

— Improves eye health

— Reduces blood pressure levels

TOMATOES

—Prevents cells from damage with lycopene

—Vitamin B, & E

—Protects eyes

—Protects lungs

—Oral Health

—May prevent skin cancer

WHITE ONIONS

—Blood thinner

—Heart health

—Promotes sleep quality

—Antibacterial properties

—Helps prevents cancer

Sauteed Green Vegetables in water

(***continued***)

GARLIC

—Anti-inflammatory

—Antioxidant

—Boosts immunity

—Heart health

—Regulates blood pressure

—Clears skin

—Garlic oil is good for sore joints.

BOK CHOY

—Cruciferous, green leafy vegetable

—Rich in C, A, K, folate

—Good source of minerals, such as calcium, phosphorus, and potassium

—Good for strong, healthy bones

—Helps reduce inflammation

GREEN DRINK

GREEN DRINK

(*continued*)

SPINACH

Rich in many nutrients, including vitamin A, vitamin C, iron, folate, and potassium.

Spinach is full of fiber.

APPLESAUCE

Applesauce has antioxidants that may reduce your risk of cancer, diabetes, and heart disease.

Using fresh apple sauce with whole fruit, including skin, helps to ensure that you get the most antioxidants possible.

Use organic apples, only, if you use whole apples.

Wash thoroughly, first.

ALMOND MILK

Almond milk, unsweetened, doesn't raise blood sugar.

Almonds are anti-cancerous.

Almond milk strengthens bones, reduces heart disease,

contains vitamin D and is dairy free.

FRUIT DRINK ("SMOOTHIE")

FRUIT DRINK, "SMOOTHIE" (*continued*)

PINEAPPLE

Vitamin C, calcium, iron, riboflavin, Vitamin B6, pantothenic acid, thiamin, anti-inflammatory Pineapple is good for digestion, potassium, and is anti-arthritic.

STRAWBERRY

— Vitamin C, flavonoids, fiber, potassium, flavonoids,

heart-cardiovascular benefits

PEACHES

— High in fiber and Vitamin A

Minerals in peaches have beneficial plant compounds like antioxidants, which can help prevent aging and disease.

MANGO

—Mangoes are low in calories, yet high in nutrients, especially Vitamin C, which aids in immunity, and has great iron absorption, cell growth and repair.

BANANAS

— Bananas are a good source of several vitamins and minerals, especially potassium, Vitamin B6, and Vitamin C

PEANUT BUTTER

— Protein, carbs, fat

JASMINE GREEN TEA

(GREEN TEA)

Benefits Brain function, weight reduction,

skin inflammation, heart health,

high concentration of antioxidants

JASMINE

Rich in antioxidants that interacts with

gastrointestinal enzymes to facilitate better

nutrient absorption and promote healthy

bowel function. Eliminates harmful bacteria in the gut.

Jasmine symbolizes purity,

confidence, sensuality, modesty,

inspiration, calm, and happy vibes.

(Cup and saucer bought in Thailand,

Bangkok by Ms. Khalidah Kali.)

HIBISCUS TEA

NUTRITIONAL VALUES AND A FEW DIFFERENT NAMES FOR HIBISCUS TEA

LOWERS BLOOD PRESSURE

STRENGTHENS IMMUNE SYSTEM

SUPPORTS LIVER HEALTH

RICH AND PROTECTIVE WITH ANTIOXIDANTS

SUCH AS VITAMIN C, WHICH HAS A
WIDE SPECTRUM OF HEALING

FIGHTS INFLAMMATION

LOWERS CHOLESTEROL

PROMOTES WEIGHT LOSS

HIBISCUS TEA IS KNOWN BY MANY NAMES:

BISSOP – IN SENEGAL, & WEST AFRICA

JAMAICA--IN MEXICO AND SPANISH-SPEAKING
COUNTRIES

SORREL – IN BARBADOS & CARIBBEAN ISLANDS

SOBOLO – IN GHANA

ZOBO -- IN NIGERIA

KARKADE -- IN NORTH AFRICA, EGYPT, & SUDAN

(Used in rituals to manifest love, et cetera.)

(Helped Africa survive psychologically & spiritually.)

OTHER HERBAL TEA FAVORITES
AND HEALTH BENEFITS

Don't rely on information as a substitute for professional medical advice, diagnosis, treatment, professional counseling, or care,

VALERIAN

Excellent for insomnia and relaxation.

CHAMOMILE

Relieves stress and anxiety, sleep, skin conditions, anti-inflammatory, anti-spasmodic properties.

PEPPERMINT

Caffeine-free, digestion, tension headaches and migraines, relieves menstrual cramps, improves sleep, calming and refreshing beautiful feeling.

SENNA

Constipation and weight loss.

(Very effective! Use with caution!)

CASCARA SAGRADA

Stimulates the bowel and has a laxative effect.

(Very effective! Use with caution!)

HERBAL ACTIONS

Concepts, suggestions, and techniques outlined are not intended as a substitute for professional health care and medical advice.

Application of any ideas and information contained in this book is at the reader's sole discretion and risk.

"And God said, "Behold, I have given you every herb bearing seed, which is upon the face of the earth, and every tree, in which is the fruit of a tree yielding seed: to you it shall be for food." Genesis 1:29

HERBAL ACTIONS

* SPIRITUALIZE *   TRANQUILIZE   * HEAL*

* PROTECT   * BEAUTIFY *

SPIRITUALIZE

Sage

Sandalwood

Myrrh & Frankincense

Peppermint

Garlic

Cedar

Rosemary

Lavender

Jasmine

TRANQUILIZE

Lavender

Sandalwood

Catnip

Chamomile

Clary Sage

Sage

Ylang-Ylang

(*TRANQUILIZE* - CONTINUED)

Cedar

Motherwort

Skullcap

Wood Betony

Dandelion, Nettle, Rose

H E A L

Dandelion

Yarrow

Sheppard's Purse

Nettle

Kelp (Anti-Carcinogenic)

Garlic (Anti-Carcinogenic)

St. John's Wort

Red Clover

Red Raspberry

Eucalyptus

Evening Primrose

P R O T E C T

Garlic

Khus Khus

St. John's Wort

(*PROTECT* – *continued*)

Rosemary

Eucalyptus

Cumin

Peppermint

Myrrh & Frankincense

Sage is also good for wisdom and intuition.

BEAUTIFY

Seaweeds (Kelp)

Youth Oil

(Aloe Vera & 10 Drops Lavender)

Rose

Nettle

Dandelion

Vitamin E

Chlorophyll

Lavender

Ylang Ylang

Sage

Rosemary

*VARIOUS HERBAL USAGES AND METHODS

* (**NOTE**: You must research usages and methods, first.)

Essential Oils

Aromatherapy

Inhaling (With Prayers & Vision)

Smudging

Decoction

Potpourri

Burn

Stir-fry

Bath

Soup

Lotion

Incense

Cotton Ball

Tincture

Syrup

Vinegars,

Salves, Lozenge, Liquid, Spray

Diffuser, Tablet, Capsule

Herbal Usages and Methods are Endless.

Please check "Books and Resources" Page near back of this book, plus Internet for recommended books on Herbal Usages and Methods.

AFFIRMATIONS

(An affirmation is emotional support and encouragement.)

"Words saturated with sincerity, conviction, faith, and intuition shatter the rocks of difficulties, and create the change desired." Paramahansa Yogananda

Khalidah Kali at an outdoor temple in India.

AFFIRMATIONS

Today, I am being devoted to being miracle-minded,

and miraculously blessed.

Be yourself but be your best self.

Everybody is a star.

Be blessed and be a blessing.

Drink half your weight in ounces of water.

Your mind is divine. Your body is divine.

You are in divine order.

Spiritual breakthrough is speeded by deliberate dispossession.

A kiss is not a promise.

I live in peace and harmony, and the universe supports me.

Love is its own reward.

Love is the means, and the end.

God is peace. Resign yourself to the infinite peace within you.

Everybody wants to shine.

You are 20 feet tall.

Construct a mind palace.

Any situation is transformed into perfection when you apply love.

I love you. Sorry. Please forgive me. /My body is my temple and alter.

My home is my sanctuary. My words and actions are my prayers.

AFFIRMATIONS - (CONTINUED)

Psalms 23

Another day; another blessing

The best, and the blessed must be willing to help the rest.

Do your best, and let God do the rest.

Pretty is not an accomplishment.

Beauty is a spirit.

Minimize consumption. Maximize wellness.

See it to see it. Seek it to see it.

Be blessed and be a blessing.

Intelligence and perfection are not a skill. It's an attitude.

Your attitude determines your altitude.

She who knows she has enough is rich.

What I am seeking is also seeking me, therefore, I am mindful of what I think, believe, say, and do.

To have what we want is riches, but to do without is power.

True affluence is not needing anything.

It takes just a little extra effort to be above average.

I will not give my power away with anger, jealousy, laziness, worry, lateness, bitterness, and general self-sabotage.

God is in the blessings business, and I am in business with God.

You are too blessed to be stressed. The best is yet to come.

BOOKS AND RESOURCES

KHALIDAH KALI, AUTHOR

"Exquisite Egyptian 'Belly' Dance Moves,

Fun * Fitness * Femininity"

Founder and Artistic Director,

Khalidah's North African Dance Experience Inc.,
a Not-For-Profit 501(c)(3) organization

A beautiful dance company performing traditional and contemporary north African dance styles with company and solo performances for weddings, and special events.

We're based in Chicago, Illinois, USA, however we do travel.

We also provide resources for Women's Advocacy.

Donate now at khalidahsdance.com, or write at khalidah@att.net

(**BOOKS AND RESOURCES** *continued*)

Chicago, Illinois - USA

Khalidah@att.net

www.Khalidahsdance.com

(For classes and full spectrum of information)

In-Person and on-line dance classes.

Khalidah has instructional dance videos available for

purchase, hard copy or virtually.

Please email to inquire before purchasing.

Email: Khalidah@att.net

CashApp: $Khalidahkali77

Zelle: khalidah@att.net

RECOMMENDED BOOKS

-- "You asked Aunt Rocky:

Answers & Advice

About Raqs Sharqi & Raqs Shaabi"

By Morocco (C. Varga Dinicu) --

"Belly Dance with Shalimar Ali" Middle Eastern Dance Book

BOOKS AND RESOURCES

(*continued*)

--Instructional Dance Books by Zarifah Aradon

--"Grandmother's Secrets"

The Ancient Rituals and Healing Power of Belly Dancing

By Rosina-Fawi

(Herstory of women's dancing, and story of author's
coming-of-age in the Arab world.)

--All books and videos by Tamalyn Dallal emerald-dreams.com

--"Life in Motion" and "Ballerina Body"

Both books by Misty Copeland

--"The Magic in Food"

By Scott Cunningham

--"The Belly Dance Book" By Tazz Richards

--"Magical Aromatherapy" By Cunningham

"Complete Book of Herbs" By Courage Books

--"Wise Woman Herbal" and "Healing Wise" By Susan Weed

--"Prescription for Nutritional Healing" By Phyllis A. Balch

--"Dressed to Kill" By Sydney Ross Singer and Soma Grismaijer

A FEW FAVORITE DANCE TEACHERS

ARTISTS IN NORTH AFRICAN & MIDDLE EASTERN DANCE
(A few mentioned in "Books" above.)

--"Morocco" C. Varga Dinicu of New York

www.casbahdance.org

--Tarik the Sultan of New York, Male Dancer Extraordinaire

--Tito of Egypt, Male Dancer Extraordinaire

--Hamza El Din, Souheir Zaki, Fifi Abdu, Nagwa Fouad;

  All in immediate above line from Egypt & so many more!

--All teachings/videos by Jamilla & Fatima Al-Wahid

https://jamillaalwahid.com

--Mama Somra of St. Louis

  jdgarmac@yahoo.com

--Sofiyah Bailey of Hollywood, Florida

Cultural Expressions

njerisofiyah@hotmail.com

culturalexpressions1love@gmail.com

--Najwa Dance Corps of Chicago, Illinois

West African Dance & All Dance Styles!

www.najwadance.org

BELOVED DANCE TEACHERS:

--Darlene Blackburn, Chicago, IL

darlene.blackburn@yahoo.com

--Joel Hall Dance Center, Chicago, Illinois

Joel Hall, Founder & Artistic Director

www.joelhall.org

--Natya Dance Theatre, Chicago, Illinois

Hema Rajagopolan,

Founder & Artistic Director

www.natya.com

--All teachings/videos by

Horacio and Beata Cifuentes

oriental-fantasy.com

A FEW FAVORITE EGYPTIAN SINGERS/MUSIC

—Hamza El Din (Nubian Baba-King)

—Ali Farka Toure'

—Om Kalthoum

—Hossam Ramzy

A FEW FAVORITE EGYPTIAN SINGERS/MUSIC
(Continued)

—Abdul Halim Hafez

—Farid El Altrache'

—Warda

—Natacha Atlas

—Ahmed Adaweia

TRADE PUBLICATION:

HABIBI

(There are many others.)

VIDEOS:

--Khalidah Kali's dance instructional videos

--allaboutbellydance.com

--Ramzy Music International

hossamramzy.com

(Vintage Egyptian videos/music - Does not disappoint!)

MORE RECOMMENDED BOOKS!

"Sacred Woman" & all books by Queen Afua

"Women's Bodies-Women's Wisdom," Christiane Northrop

"Wine of the Mystic – Paramahansa Yogananda

"The Prosperity Bible" Napoleon Hill, et al/All Louise Hay Books

SUPPLIERS:

--Dahlal International

St. Louis, MO

800-745-6432

dahlal.com

(Costumes, accessories, music videos)

--Turquois International

Woodland Hills, CA 91367

818-999-5542 or 800-548-9422

turquoisinternational.com

(Costumes, videos, accessories,

cymbals, music, videos)

--www.saroyancymbals.com

SKETCHES OF MOVEMENTS

BY MS. BRIDGET HOWARD OF
CHICAGO, ILLINOIS (USA)

Chest Drop

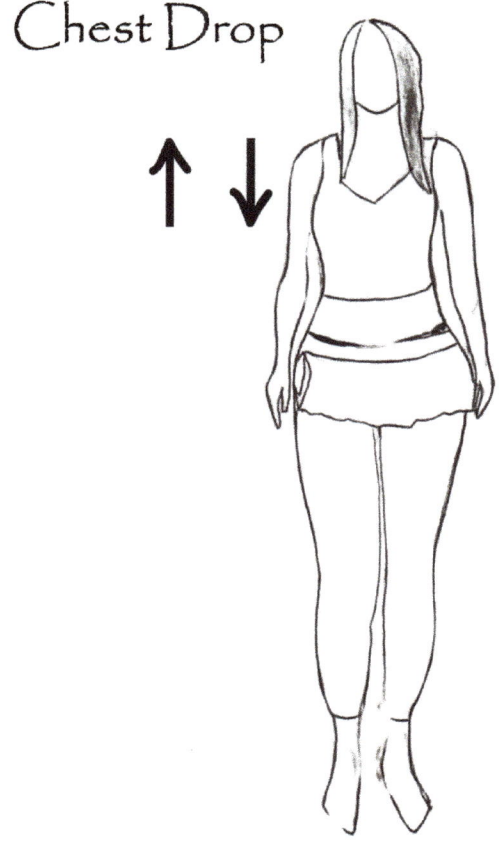

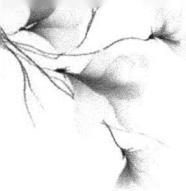

Chest Lift

Chest Quiver

Chest Lift
with Quiver

Chest Slide

Chest Slide with Quiver

Figure 8
(Forward)

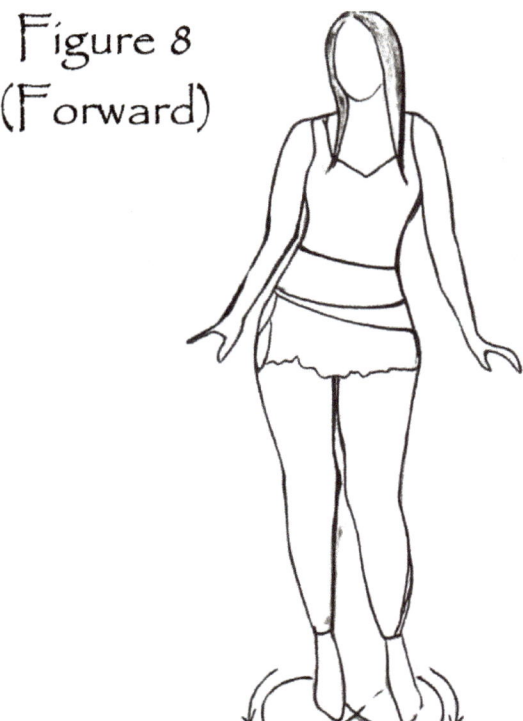

Figure 8
(Backward)

Hip Quiver

Ferris Wheel
Hip

Hip Lift

Hip Drop

Hip Slide

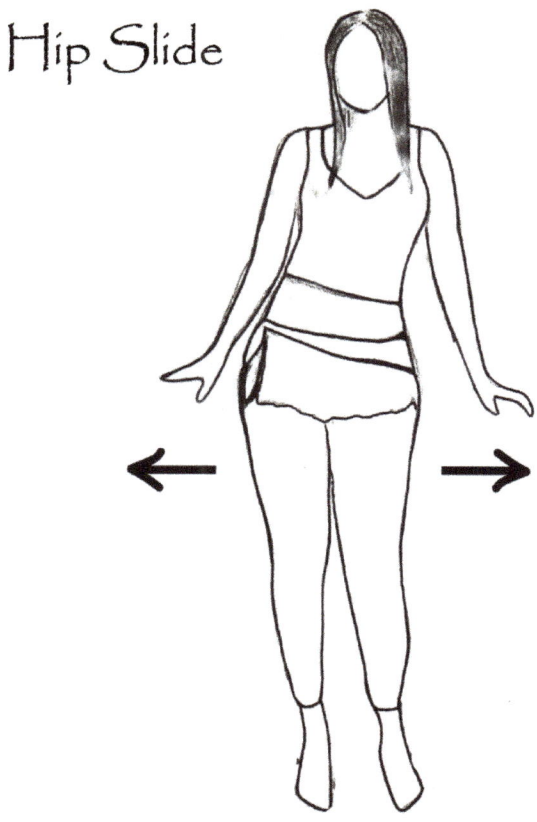

Hip Slide with Quiver

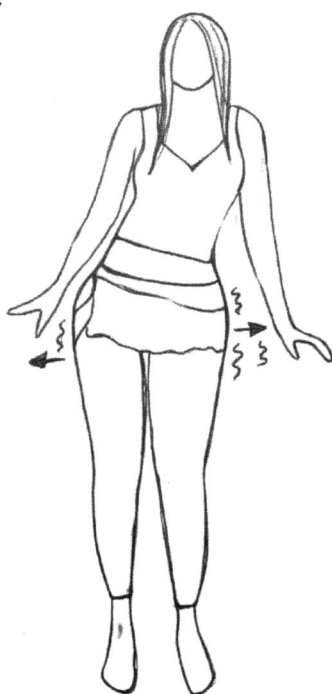

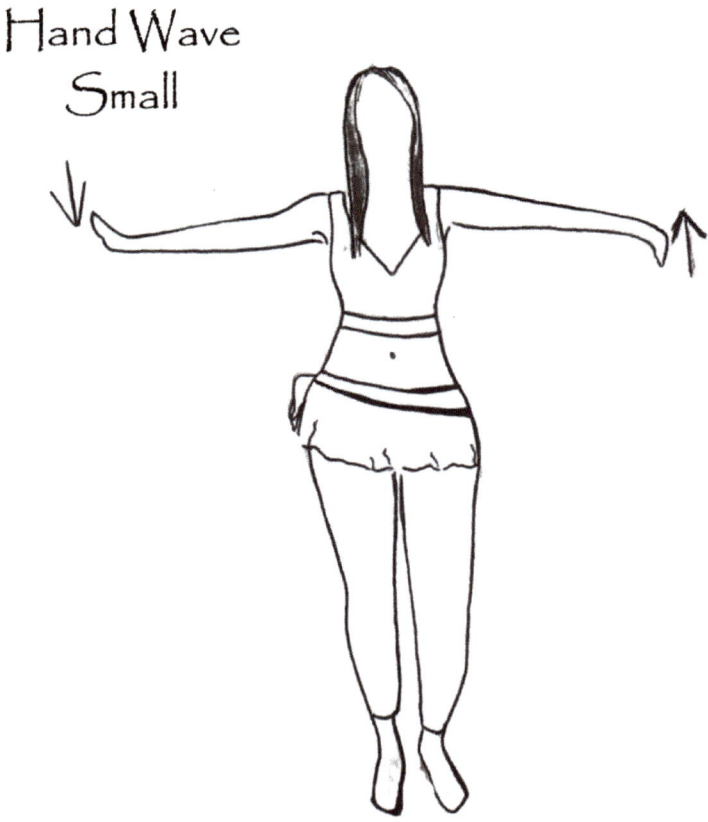

Hand Wave
Small

Hand Wave
Large

Pelvic Arch

Pelvic Circle

Pelvic Circle
with Quiver

Pelvic
Contraction

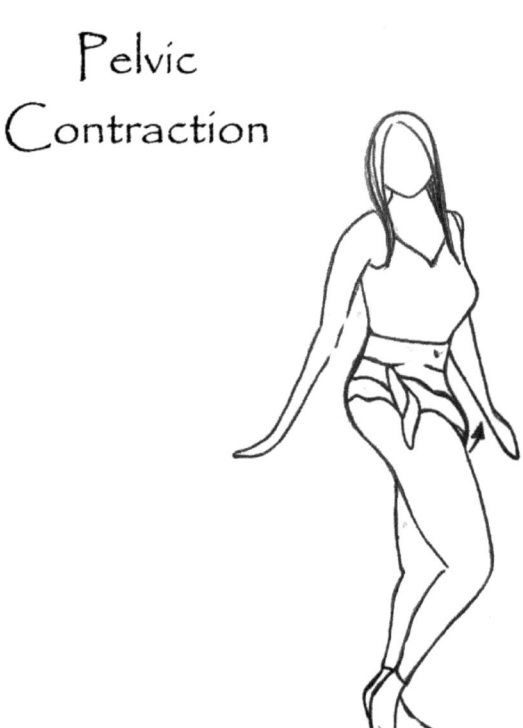

Pelvic Wave
with Quiver 2

Hip Quiver
Walk

Torso Wave 1

Torso Wave 2

Horizontal Arm
Wave
Small

Horizontal Arm
Wave
Large

ABOUT THE AUTHOR

Giving praises to The Most High for capability and truthfulness of all information herein, etcetera.

Daughter, Sister, Mother, Grandmother, God Mother, Dance Mother, Aunt, Cousin, Niece (Born in poverty and borderline homelessness within a culture of domestic violence …….)

"Khalidah is a native Chicagoan, USA.

Graduate of Jones Commercial High School and

Chicago College of Commerce.

In college, Khalidah received scholarship funding based on her childhood story.

"Khalidah retired (Graduated & Ascended) after 37 years of service, full-time, as an Illinois Board examined, Licensed, and Certified Official Court Reporter, (Court Stenographer)

In 2024, Khalidah authored a book, "Exquisite Egyptian

'Belly' Dance Moves, * Fun * Fitness * Femininity"

(ABOUT THE AUTHOR)

Khalidah has been extremely influenced by, and in debt to the following personal dance teachers and leaders:

--The Late Jewel McLaurin, Chicago, IL

--Mama Najwa, Founder of

Najwa Dance Corps, Chicago

--Darlene Blackburn, Chicago, IL

--"Morocco" C. Varga Dinicu of New York City

--Master Danny Diallo Hinds

Ayotunde Productions

Multi-Arts and Culture Agency

Barbados, West Indies, Caribbean &

Kansas City, Missouri

--Somra El Nubia (June Maclin)

St. Louis, Missouri

--Sofiyah Bailey, Cultural Expressions,

Hollywood, Florida; St. Louis, Missouri; and Chicago, IL

--Joel Hall Center & Joel Hall Dancers

Chicago, IL

ABOUT THE AUTHOR)

(Personal Dance Leaders/Teachers)

--Master, Yirser Ra Hotep of Yogaskills, Chicago IL

--Hema Rajagopalan, Natya Dance Center

Chicago, IL

--Mama Amaniyea, Emeritus,

Executive Director

Muntu Dance Theatre

--Homer Bryant,

Founder and Artistic Director,

Chicago Multi-Cultural Dance Center

--Delia Tyler, Scholar

Dancer and Artist Extraordinaire

--Moveme Soul,

Ayesha Jaco, Artistic Director

--Khalidah performed The Hajj twice! (Islamic Pilgrimage)

Khalidah has traveled over 45 countries worldwide

with travel emphasis in Africa and Asia.

--Khalidah traveled Egypt over a dozen times on

Black studies and dance study-focused trips.

--Recently traveled Asia: Thailand, Singapore, Malaysia, And Dubai

(ABOUT THE AUTHOR)

CERTIFICATIONS:

— Certified Kemetic Yoga Instructor by Master, Yiser Ra Hotep

— Certified Holistic Health Consultant

  (Institute of Integrative Nutrition, New York)

—. Certified Birth Labor Doula

— Certified Zumba Instructor

— Certified Creating Herbal Medicine & Plant Identification

— Certified in stage and print modeling

__Certified with Advanced Metaphysical Studies by

  Dr. Delbert Blair, Chicago, "The Meta Center"

Etcetera

Khalidah's great-grandfather, Elijah P. Marrs (1840–1910), founded an HBCU in Louisville, Kentucky, that remains active to this day. In addition, he established Beargrass Missionary Baptist Church in 1880, which is also still active, and has written an autobiography in his name, Elijah P. Marrs.

ABOUT THE AUTHOR

(*continued*)

VOLUNTEERISM:

—— Khalidah has volunteered over 300 hours as a "Feeder-Rocker" at LaRabida Children's Hospitals in Chicago, Illinois, USA.

—— Khalidah founded a group of professional panelist speakers from the Judiciary, Clergy, Chicago Police Department, City Colleges of Chicago, Nurse Professionals, Attorneys and Professional Women's Advocates to speak on awareness of domestic violence and breast cancer awareness.

---Recently, Khalidah traveled to Haiti as a Certified Birth Labor Doula giving care and compassion to 20+ women during birth labor; assisting in a mobile/traveling medical unit to assist in prenatal care; offering Yoga, dance & exercise to a local orphanage.

— Khalidah answers phones at a Telephone Prayer Line Ministry, offering prayers to callers at Apostolic Church of God (Chicago, IL)

"OTHER" INTERESTS

--Khalidah acquired an interest in dance when she won a block club party dance contest at 11 years old.

--In her early 20s, Khalidah danced in a dance contest for 11 hours straight!

--Khalidah always had a propensity to write, having written a daily diary from ages 11 to 18 in a home where no one was reading, writing, and with no books around.

She now has 2,000+ books in personal library.

ABOUT THE AUTHOR

(*continued*)

Khalidah started studying dance at the Jewel McLaurin School of Dance as a teenager, studying, west African dance, calypso, ballet, and modern dance, et cetera.

Started studying north African and Middle Eastern dance in 1981, non-stop to present, and has studied with over 40 dance teachers in this genre abroad and domestically.

Khalidah taught Egyptian dance at Joel Hall Dance Center for

23 years, and at Washington Park District, 23+ years to present.

Khalidah founded a dance company,

Khalidah's North African Dance Experience, Inc., began in 1986, and is a registered Not-for-Profit, tax exempt,501 (c) (3) organization.

Please, Donate Now!   Khalidahsdance.com

KNADE (Khalidah's North African Dance Experience, Inc.) has performed for over 300 corporate, and educational institutions as well as weddings, private parties, and outdoor festivals, with many performances at the annual African Festival of the Arts, Chicago.

KNADE has received awards, grants, and acknowledgments in the corporate, arts, and educational community.

KNADE has been recognized by the Office of Cultural Affairs, Department of Fine Arts, now known as Department of Cultural Affairs, Special Events (DCASE), and many other significant art institutions.

Please visit khalidahsdance.com for further information.

ABOUT THE AUTHOR

(*continued*)

Khalidah is a Dance-Teacher-Favorite at the Belly Dancers of Color (BOCA) Convention in Washington, D. C.

Khalidah loves God, dance, exercise, Yoga, reading, writing, traveling, gourmet cooking, gardening, choreographing dances, loving people, and loving life; always in a positive mindset, and loves collecting positive affirmations.

She performs her movements exquisitely, with a beautiful peacefulness and ageless beauty!

Her classes are: "A Temple of Dance & Wellness."

Khalidah lives in Chicago with Wonderful Husband,

Theodore Evans.

www.khalidahsdance.com

www.khalidahstempleofwellness.com

khalidah@att.net

Khalidah's North African Dance Experience, Inc., provides a safe and happy space to learn and dance.

Khalidah's work is being installed virtually at
The Chicago Dance History Project and at
The Newberry Library in Chicago, Illinois USA.

www.ingramcontent.com/pod-product-compliance
Lightning Source LLC
Chambersburg PA
CBHW051200120626
46547CB00012B/1139